# THE FAT RAT WITH NO HAT

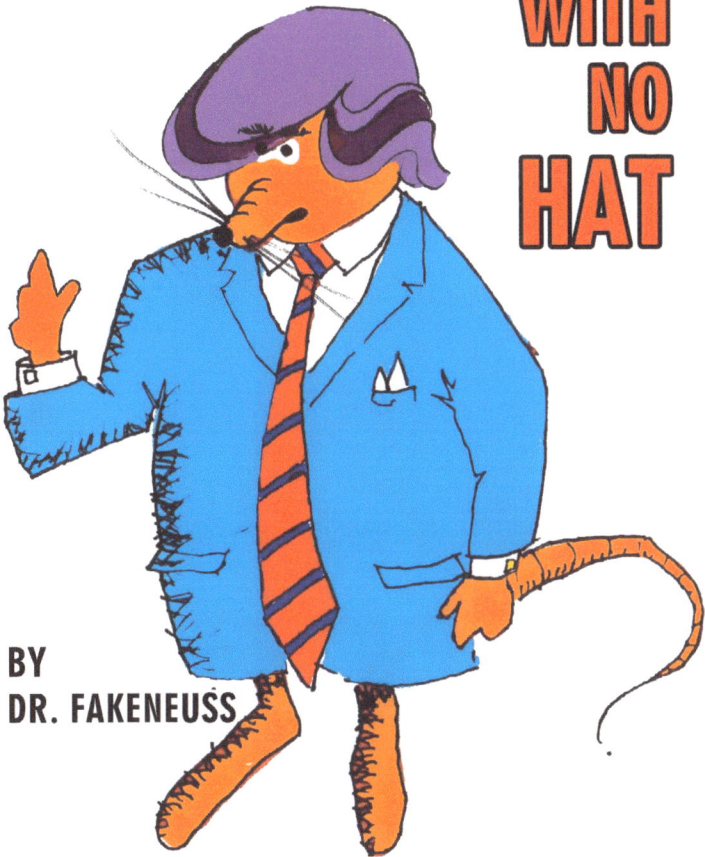

BY
DR. FAKENEUSS

DORRANCE
PUBLISHING CO
EST. 1920
PITTSBURGH, PENNSYLVANIA 15238

Dorrance Publishing Co
585 Alpha Drive
Suite 103
Pittsburgh, PA 15238
Visit our website at *www.dorrancebookstore.com*

ISBN: 978-1-6461-0626-4
eISBN: 978-1-6461-0096-5

# THE FAT RAT WITH NO HAT

BY
DR. FAKENEUSS

A pall had descended;
It was all wet and soggy.
Depressing and dim,
Life was darkness and foggy.

Mother had left;
She wasn't around.
She was out running errands,
Buying groceries downtown.

There was nothing to do, so
We sat, and we stared.
I stared with Maria
As we sat in our chairs.

We sat, and we stared,
With plenty of cares.
We sat, and we sat,
And we stared with our cares.

We looked out the window
As it rained dogs and cats,
And up the front walk
Came a fat rat with no hat.

His hair, it was purple,
His tie long and red.
The suit looked like silk.
He had a big head.

4

He came to the door
Without knock or a ring.
He entered the house
Like he owned the whole thing.

With lips that were curled,
And small fingers a-twitter.
He said now we're his guests,
And we'd better know better.

"I see that you're scared,"
He sneered as he said,
"Don't worry a bit—
There's nothing to dread!"

"My name's Don LaCon,
And you'll have a great time.
We'll do the hugest of things
Without causing crimes."

"I'll make everything perfect;
It will all be great fun.
First, we'll spruce up the house
And give everyone guns."

"I have plenty of weapons
To shoot up the place."
*(I thought Mother would think
That this was a disgrace.)*

6

7

"We need guns everywhere:
In churches and schools,
In courthouses, theaters,
And restaurants and pools."

"They will keep us all safe,
All the time—have no fear.
We need them on hand
Every day of the year."

He shot holes in the ceiling,
The couch, and the bed.
"Don't worry about bullets
Flying right past your head."

"Guns and ammo are good.
As good as it gets.
If we all shoot some more,
We can make more bull-ets."

So, this rat in our midst,
With the purplest of hair,
Acted as if
We weren't even there.

11

"Maria," said I,
"This doesn't look good.
When mother gets home,
We'll be misunderstood."

He put on a crown
From a cheap burger joint.
Then found my toy sword
And did thus self-anoint.

With a most royal pretense,
He called himself "King."
Then took a tub bath
That left a black ring.

"Don't worry about
All the coal and the oil.
The tub's too pristine,
It needs to be soiled."

"This house is too clean,
And no one will care
If we pollute water,
The carpet, and air:"

When I asked him to stop,
He replied most reflexive;
He spat vitriol
With the vilest invective.

"If you correct me, look out!
I'll punch you right back!"
*(With this kind of outlook,
We'll be blue and all black.)*

He turned up the heat
'Til the house was ablaze.
Ice cubes were melting
Inside of their trays.

14

Energy's cheap;
Use as much as you can.
Utility stocks
Need be frantically fanned.

Ice cream was flowing
All over the floor.
The freezer hung open,
As well as fridge doors.

15

He took all our pinwheels
And crushed them with glee.
"The noise causes cancer,"
He said, "Don't you see?"

"Breathe coal, smoke, and soot
If you want healthy lives.
Fill your lungs full of gunk...
If you want to survive."

"There's no global warming;
That's just a big hoax.
A Chinese invention,
 A prank and a joke."

Next he built a great wall
With my blocks and my toys.
He said it would keep out
The bad girls and boys.

But Maria and I,
No bad boys could see.
But he forced us to build it,
And build it for free.

He used all my Legos,
And didn't say please,
Making his "beautiful" fence
That was taller than trees.

"The wall will be taller.
Taller than tall.
The wall will be taller,
The tallest of all."

He called us both names
As he bullied about.
When we stopped building,
He started to shout.

He shouted and pouted
And blamed everyone
When he couldn't build much
With limited funds.

20

It seemed to be easy,
Crossing this wall.
You could fly, boat, or climb...
Or maybe just crawl.

Fat Rat's words were quite simple;
His speech it was crude.
When he talked about women,
It all came out lewd.

He looked hard at Maria
With lust in his eyes.
"If you don't give me something,
It will be your demise!"

He called women fat,
Or a basket of bones.
If they weren't pageant beauties,
He sent them all home.

"I'll grab you by places
You don't even know
And treat you like dirt,"
Then he untied her bow.

He liked to make green-bucks,
Both here and about,
Exploiting the "littles,"
Making hugely amounts.

His friends had deep pockets,
The deepest of deep.
The deeper they got,
The more they did keep.

24

They said they grew jobs
With all of their cash,
But the only thing growing
Was their personal stash.

"I need to buy fuel
For my fine fleet of jets:"
*(So Fat Rat could golf
With those that jet-set.)*

I looked at Maria
As he asked me for money.
"You know he'll just waste it,
So don't give him any."

Then he grabbed at my ankles
And started to shake.
Coins started dropping
Like sprinkles on cake.

Don LaCon wanted
To make everything BIG.
He promised the world
He'd be BIGGER than BIG.

Big, BIGGER, BIGGEST.
The bigly of best.
He claimed he'd clean up
This whole worldly mess.

He bowed before tyrants
Whose skin was so fair.
They spoke a strange language,
These friends with a bear.

On bent knee he thanked them
For helping him out.
For getting "nasties" removed
From here and about.

With back-channel access
And spies in dark clothes,
They made mincemeat of others
While extorting their foes.

But our neighbors who had
Non-purpled hair
Were told they were bad
If their skin wasn't fair.

These folks who were darker,
With speech not the same,
Were kicked out of their houses
And treated with shame.

"These whatevers aren't welcome.
Move them back past the line.
They're all new invaders,
Unlike me and mine."

"They don't belong here.
They're deviants and louts—
All thieves and drug lords."
So he swept them all out.

Some friends of his came,
Waving flags from their cars.
They said hateful some-things
Under flags with crossed bars.

Don gave them a nod
As he saw them drive by.
"Get out of our 'hood,'"
To us they did cry.

The Don with a con
Was not happy, you see,
Unless he was treated
As God next to be.

He saw himself perched
In the most holy of places,
Angels singing his glory
And offering praises.

He played games with missiles;
He talked loud and harsh.
He threatened and yelled,
But it was mostly a farce.

He would bluster and fume
At the slightest offence,
While feeding his ego...
*(Which became quite immense).*

"And that is not all,"
He said with a grin.
He walked out of the house
And came in again.

And with him, they came,
Amid fanfare and pomp,
Little thing "J" and
Long-legged "I" stomped.

They stomped, and they stomped,
With fanfare and pomp.
They went everywhere
With their stomps and their romps.

Don put them in charge
*("I" looked great in her dresses).*
They hadn't a clue,
So they just made more messes.

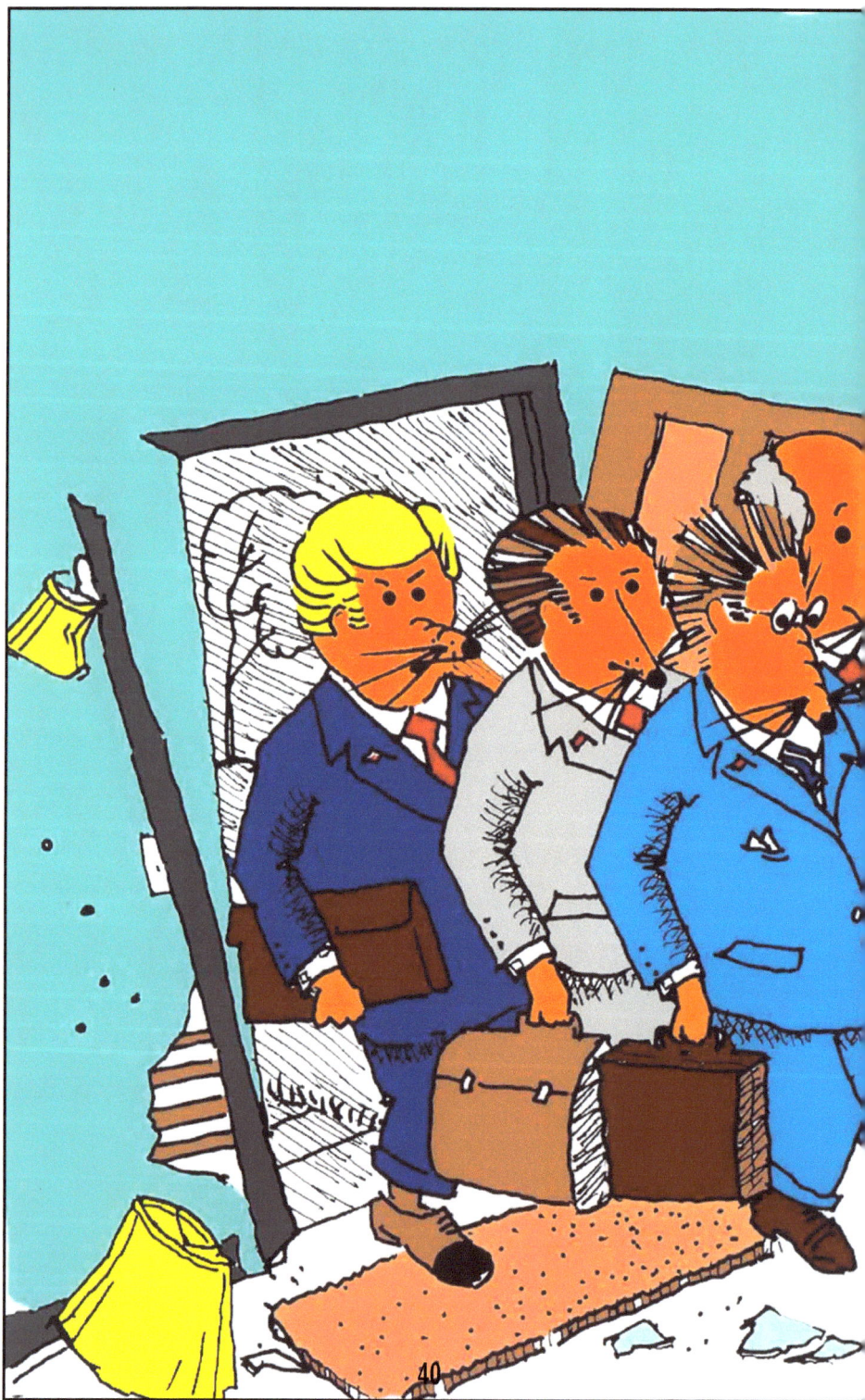

40

Then in came the big boys,
The ones with long ties.
The Rat gave them big jobs;
They were the swellest of guys.

More wealth to the wealthy,
More poor to the poor.
"To them, we'll give less,
To us, we'll give more."

They made up the rules;
They rarely got tired.
But if they crossed Don,
They were summarily fired.

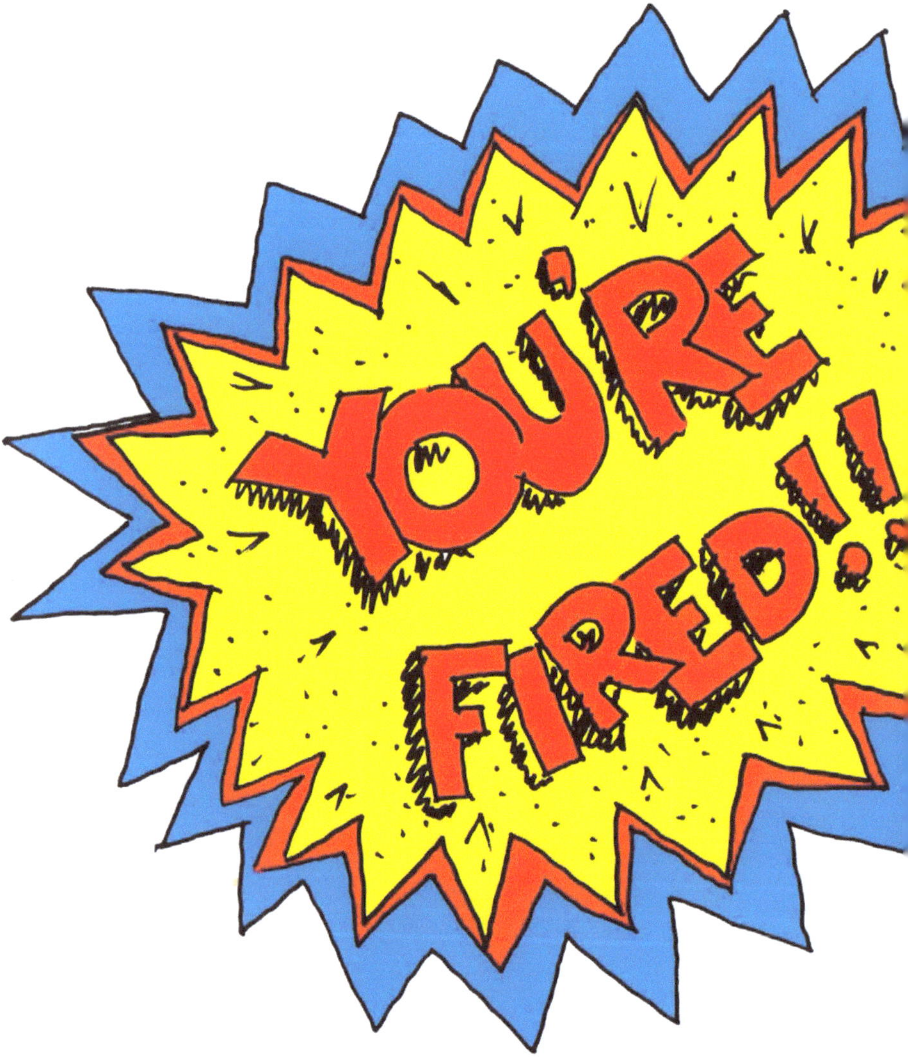
YOU'RE FIRED!!

They'd leave in disgrace,
But Fat Rat didn't care.
He'd find someone else
Right out of thin air.

The friends who were closest
Acted hearty and hale.
When caught lying for Don,
They got locked up in jail.

He had people that talked for him,
Made his heart glow.
These folks said their Rat
Was as pure as the snow.

They painted a picture
Of an upstanding rat,
Citing chapter and verse
From "Alternative Facts."

45

45

If someone said something
Don didn't approve,
He would angrily scowl
While screaming, "Fake News!"

"I'm always right,
And you're always wrong.
Your facts are all weak;
My facts are all strong."

46

"The only news you can trust
Is the stuff I make up.
Don't listen to those
Who don't drink from my cup."

He made sure that he told us,
"We are having a blast,"
'Til he saw through the window
Mother's feet coming up fast.

She stepped into the house
And saw the huge mess.
"It's not mine," said Fat Rat.
He wouldn't confess.

49

"This mess is disgusting!
It will take ages to mend.
We don't need this Fat Rat
Or his self-serving friends."

So Mother quite nicely,
Purple hair in her hand,
Put a boot to his pants...
Kicked him out of the land.

51

The rat was as filthy
As a pig in a sty;
Mother knew the deep truth
Of this rat with a tie.

"Leaders are servants,
Not pampered in pink.
They give of themselves.
Of others, they think."

Mother put us in chairs,
Where we sat and we sat.
She began to explain
Fat rats with no hats.

She said that the world
Is full of such ilk,
Who love their gold cufflinks
And suits made of silk.

"Be careful of those
Who find it easy to hate.
They will enter our lives
If we open the gate."

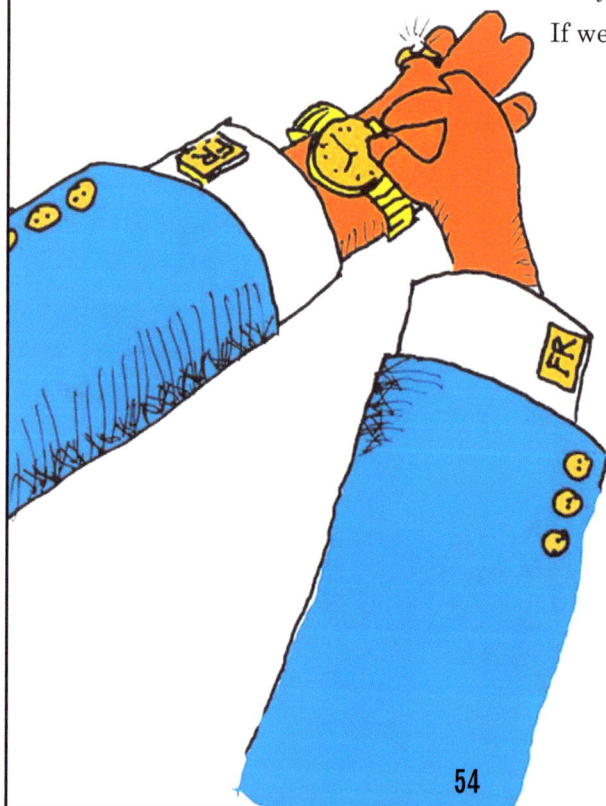

54

"Don't let violence and spite
Become the new norm,
Or we'll quickly turn into
That which we scorn."

"Lives must be nurtured
With patience and care.
Tolerance frees people,
Their talents to share."

So we sat, and we pondered,
Maria and I,
About what we're made of:
The truth or a lie.

55

The more we sat thinking,
The more it 'came clear:
Fat rats can create
A backdrop of fear.

Building walls around fortunes,
Excluding others at will,
Feeding hate in one's heart,
Treating others like swill.

This might be our end,
Should we forget we belong;
As we, too, are rats
And a part of the throng.

Because we're all given
The desire to care,
To serve and to love
With nobody spared.

We may have long whiskers,
and noses and tails.
We may come up short,
And often will fail.

But we're called to live justly,
And seek what will give
The chance for all creatures
A full life to live.

\* Fat Rat's found hat (redacted)

CPSIA information can be obtained
at www.ICGtesting.com
Printed in the USA
BVHW021309090520
578326BV00001B/10